BEADILY PATTERNS

80+

PEYOTE
BRICK STITCH

Hi my dear friends!

My name is Natalee Alex.

I am very glad that you liked my patterns.
I hope you get a great jewelry.

So, for work you need Miyuki Delika
or Toho seed beads size 10/0, 11/0
or Czech seed beads size 10/0.

Weaving method you can choose Peyote or Bricks.
This picture shows the method of weaving Bricks.

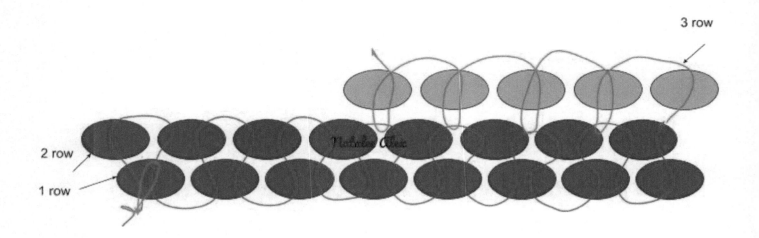

This picture shows the method of weaving Peyote.

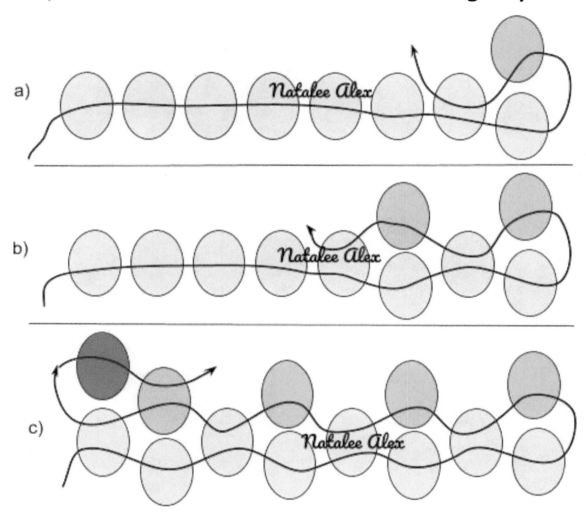

a)

b)

c)

I hope you understand these methods.
This is not difficult!
You can start weaving from anywhere.
You will definitely get a beautiful thing.
Wish you success.

If you have any questions my e-mail:
nat50ka6699@gmail.com

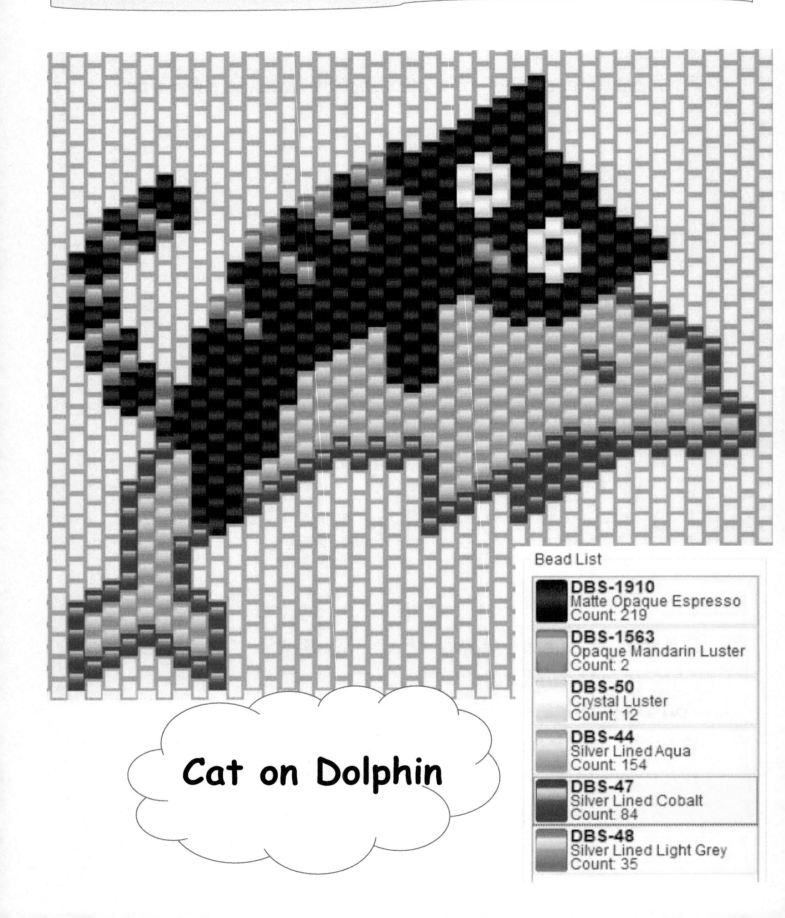

Cat on Dolphin

Bead List

	DBS-1910
	Matte Opaque Espresso
	Count: 219

	DBS-1563
	Opaque Mandarin Luster
	Count: 2

	DBS-50
	Crystal Luster
	Count: 12

	DBS-44
	Silver Lined Aqua
	Count: 154

	DBS-47
	Silver Lined Cobalt
	Count: 84

	DBS-48
	Silver Lined Light Grey
	Count: 35

Beading patterns from Natalee Alex

Panda

Bead List

	DB-10 Black Count: 848	
	DB-47 Silver Lined Cobalt Count: 6	
	DB-50 Crystal Luster Count: 483	
	DB-55 Pink Lined Crystal AB Count: 31	

Koala

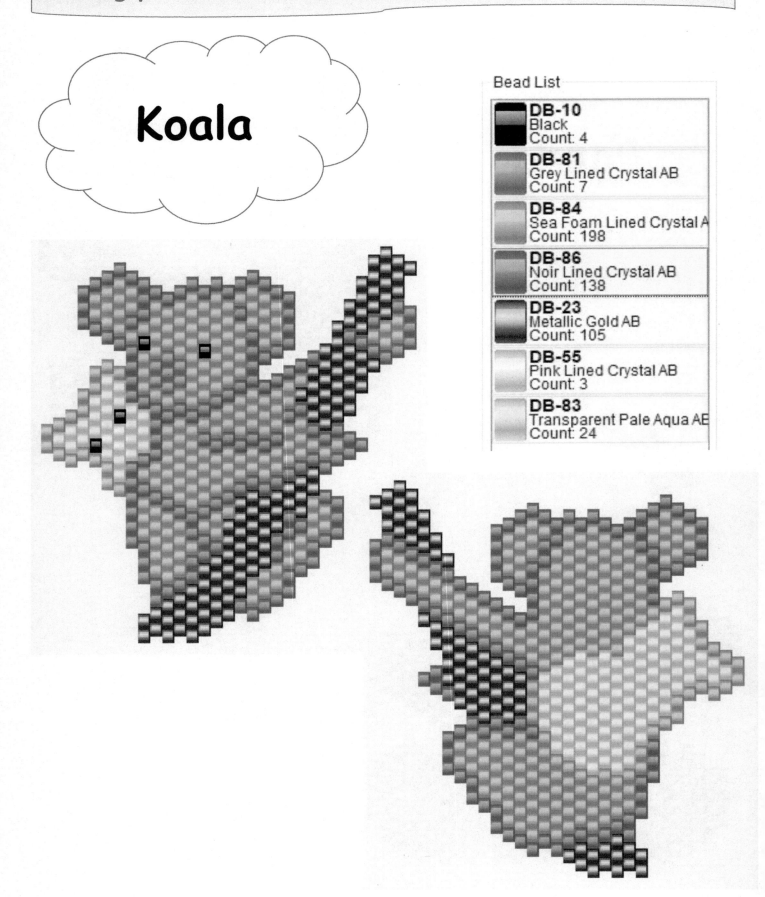

Bead List

	DB-10	Black — Count: 4
	DB-81	Grey Lined Crystal AB — Count: 7
	DB-84	Sea Foam Lined Crystal A — Count: 198
	DB-86	Noir Lined Crystal AB — Count: 138
	DB-23	Metallic Gold AB — Count: 105
	DB-55	Pink Lined Crystal AB — Count: 3
	DB-83	Transparent Pale Aqua AB — Count: 24

Bear

Bead List

	DB-42 Silver Lined Gold Count: 213
	DB-126 Cinnamon Rainbow Gold L Count: 551
	DB-710 Transparent Yellow Count: 70
	DB-10 Black Count: 10
	DB-43 Silver Lined Flame Red Count: 5
	DB-50 Crystal Luster Count: 4

Penguin

Bead List

	DB-43 Silver Lined Flame Red Count: 205	
	DB-10 Black Count: 362	
	DB-45 Silver Lined Orange Count: 94	
	DB-50 Crystal Luster Count: 205	
	DB-57 Aqua Lined Crystal AB Count: 12	

Cute tooth

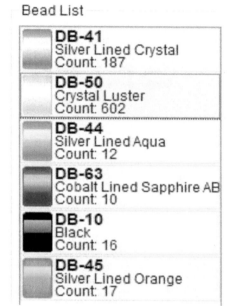

Bead List

	DB-41	Silver Lined Crystal Count: 187
	DB-50	Crystal Luster Count: 602
	DB-44	Silver Lined Aqua Count: 12
	DB-63	Cobalt Lined Sapphire AB Count: 10
	DB-10	Black Count: 16
	DB-45	Silver Lined Orange Count: 17

St. Patric Day

St. Patric Day

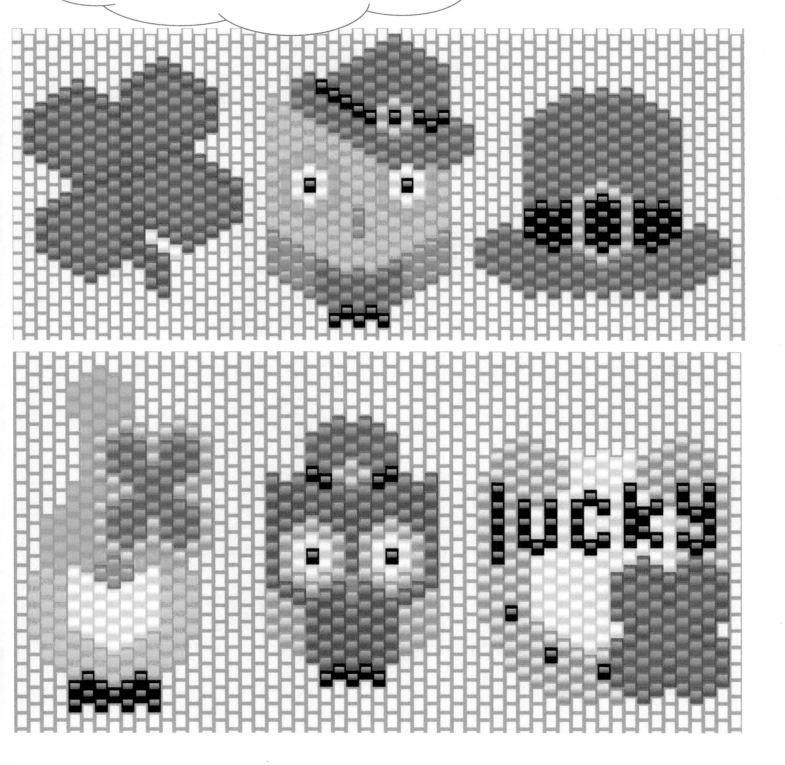

Christmas clock

Bead List

	DB-50 Crystal Luster Count: 363	
	DB-60 Lime Lined Crystal AB Count: 267	
	DB-43 Silver Lined Flame Red Count: 83	
	DB-42 Silver Lined Gold Count: 245	
	DB-10 Black Count: 77	
	DB-44 Silver Lined Aqua Count: 67	
	DB-148 Silver Lined Emerald Count: 114	

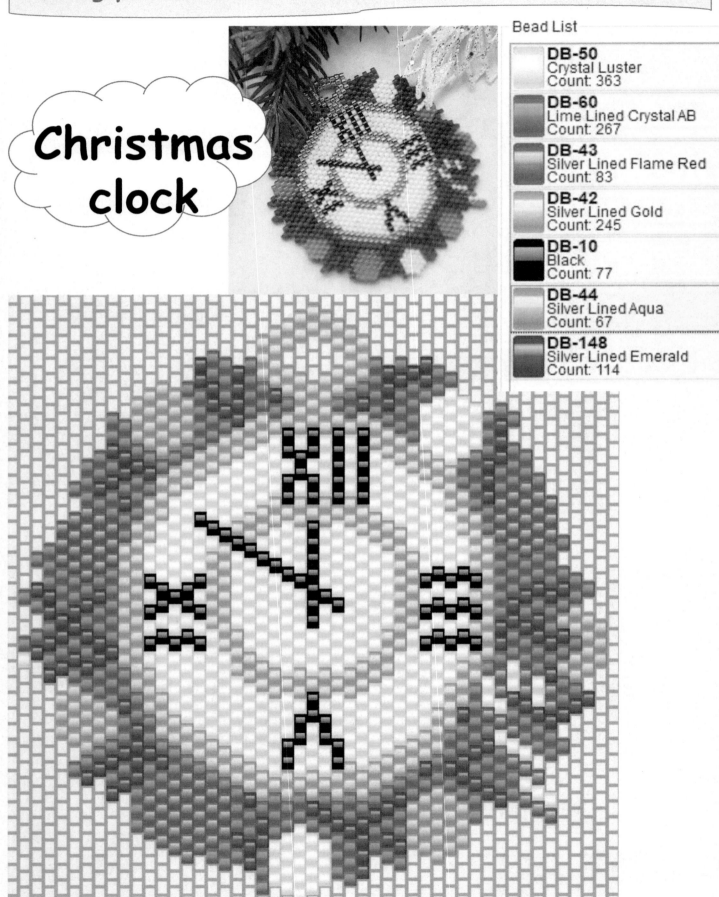

Christmas lamp

Bead List

	DB-62 Light Cranberry Lined Topaz Count: 137	
	DB-53 Light Yellow Lined Crystal A Count: 169	
	DB-61 Purple Lined Light Topaz L Count: 234	
	DB-50 Crystal Luster Count: 7	
	DB-147 Silver Lined Chartreuse Count: 87	
	DB-162 Opaque Red AB Count: 99	
	DB-148 Silver Lined Emerald Count: 67	

Nutcracker

Bead List

	DB-42 Silver Lined Gold Count: 149	
	DB-43 Silver Lined Flame Red Count: 311	
	DB-214 Opaque Red Luster Count: 145	
	DB-50 Crystal Luster Count: 280	
	DB-10 Black Count: 153	
	DB-68 Peach Lined Crystal Luster Count: 78	

Llama

Bead List

	DB-48	Silver Lined Light Grey Count: 84
	DB-50	Crystal Luster Count: 205
	DB-10	Black Count: 11
	DB-176	Transparent Aqua AB Count: 33
	DB-1226	Transparent Lime Luster Count: 55
	DB-1243	Transparent Pink Mist AB Count: 16
	DB-1301	Transparent Yellow Count: 25
	DB-1242	Transparent Dark Cranberr Count: 15

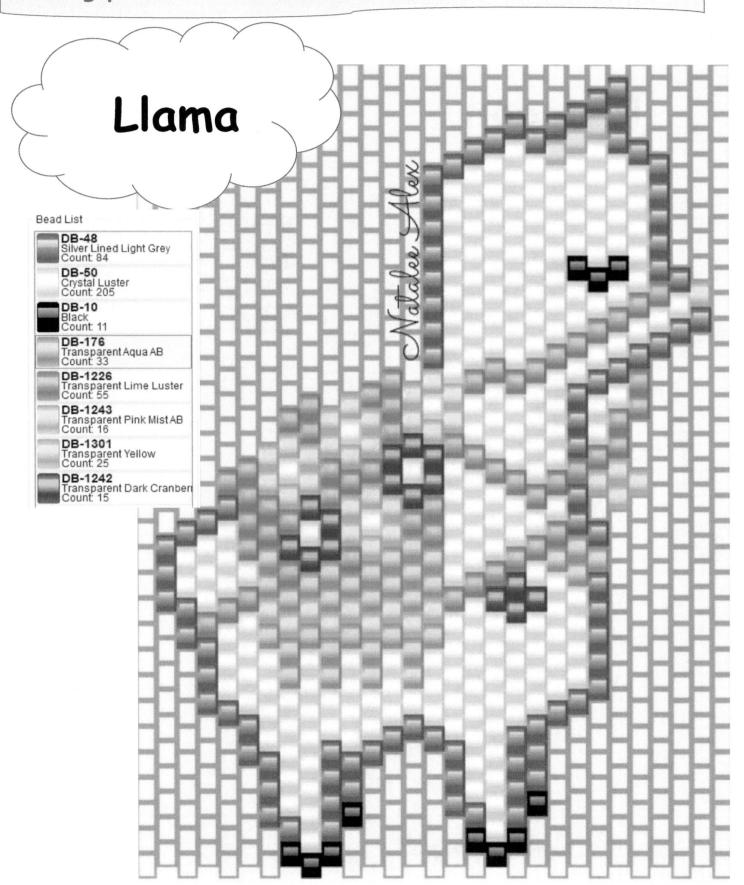

Raccoon

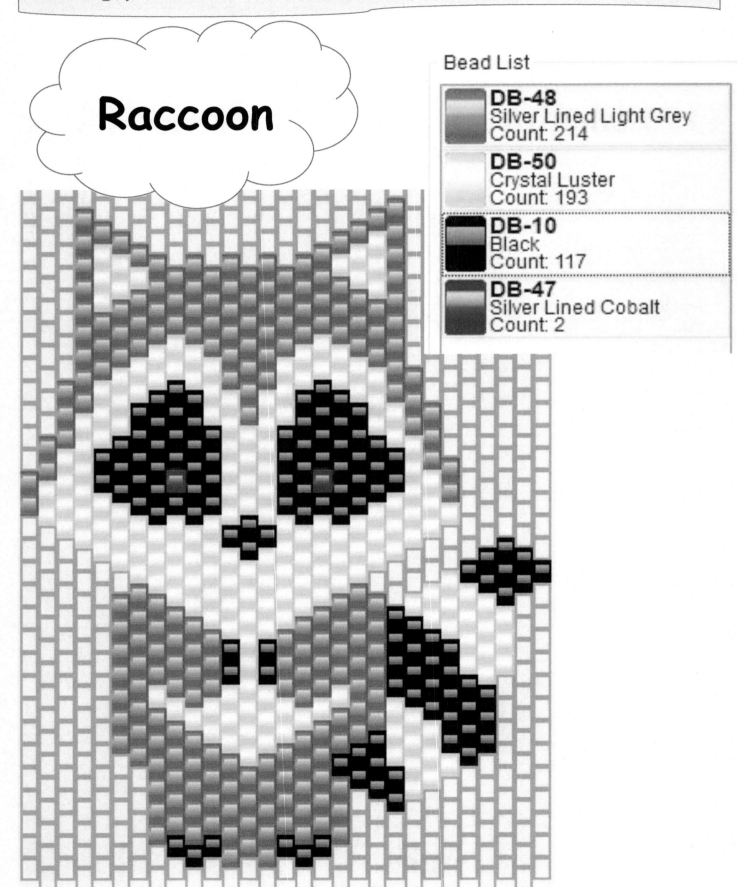

Bead List

	DB-48	Silver Lined Light Grey	Count: 214
DB-50	Crystal Luster	Count: 193
DB-10	Black	Count: 117
DB-47	Silver Lined Cobalt	Count: 2

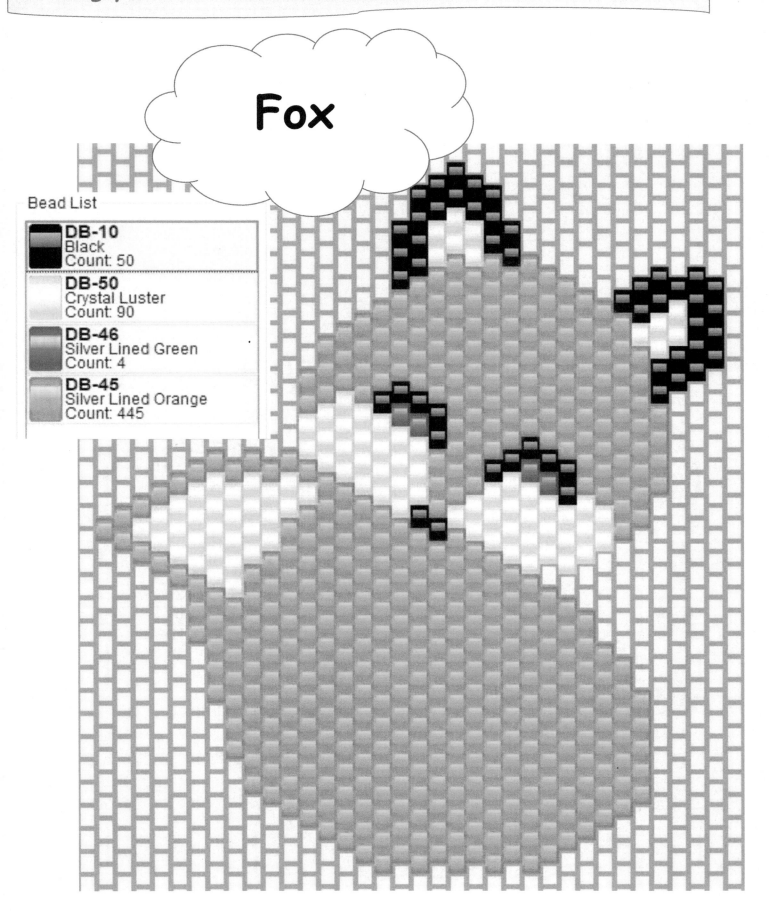

Fox

Bead List

DB-10
Black
Count: 50

DB-50
Crystal Luster
Count: 90

DB-46
Silver Lined Green
Count: 4

DB-45
Silver Lined Orange
Count: 445

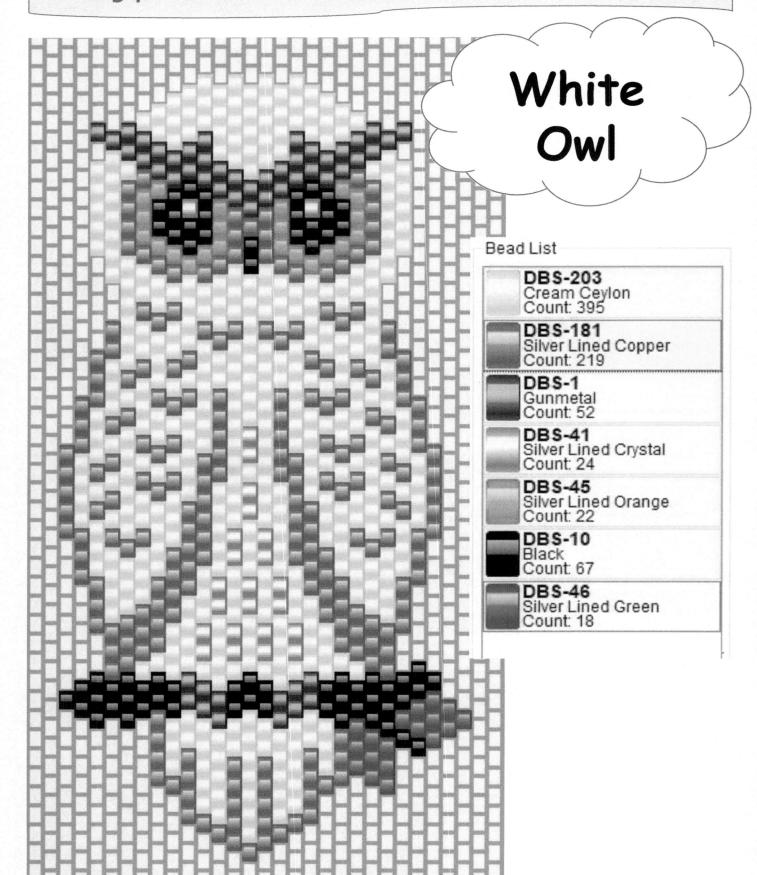

White Owl

Bead List

	DBS-203 Cream Ceylon Count: 395
	DBS-181 Silver Lined Copper Count: 219
	DBS-1 Gunmetal Count: 52
	DBS-41 Silver Lined Crystal Count: 24
	DBS-45 Silver Lined Orange Count: 22
	DBS-10 Black Count: 67
	DBS-46 Silver Lined Green Count: 18

Easter Rabbit

Bead List

	DB-42 Silver Lined Gold Count: 104	
	DB-1813 Aqua Green Satin Count: 88	
	DB-75 Dark Coral Lined Crystal A Count: 7	
	DB-74 Fuchsia Lined Crystal AB Count: 7	
	DB-82 Transparent Pale Pink AB Count: 7	
	DB-77 Blue Lined Crystal AB Count: 7	
	DB-45 Silver Lined Orange Count: 7	
	DB-50 Crystal Luster Count: 193	

Rabbit & easter egg

Bead List

	DB-78 Aqua Mist Lined Crystal L Count: 211	
	DB-106 Shell Pink Luster Count: 22	
	DB-10 Black Count: 8	
	DB-43 Silver Lined Flame Red Count: 79	
	DB-52 Pale Peach Lined Crystal Count: 80	
	DB-147 Silver Lined Chartreuse Count: 40	
	DB-151 Transparent Orange AB Count: 28	
	DB-166 Opaque Turquoise Green Count: 21	
	DB-160 Opaque Yellow AB Count: 40	
	DB-149 Silver Lined Capri Blue Count: 14	
	DB-158 Opaque Mauve AB Count: 52	
	DB-165 Opaque Cobalt AB Count: 131	
	DB-119 Transparent Honey Luster Count: 37	

Easter Truck

Bead List

	DB-231 Crystal Ceylon Count: 19	
	DB-10 Black Count: 17	
	DB-113 Transparent Blue Luster Count: 94	
	DB-721 Opaque Yellow Count: 34	
	DB-1106 Transparent Lime Count: 9	
	DB-1133 Opaque Mandarin Count: 8	
	DB-625 Rose Silver Lined Alabaste Count: 19	

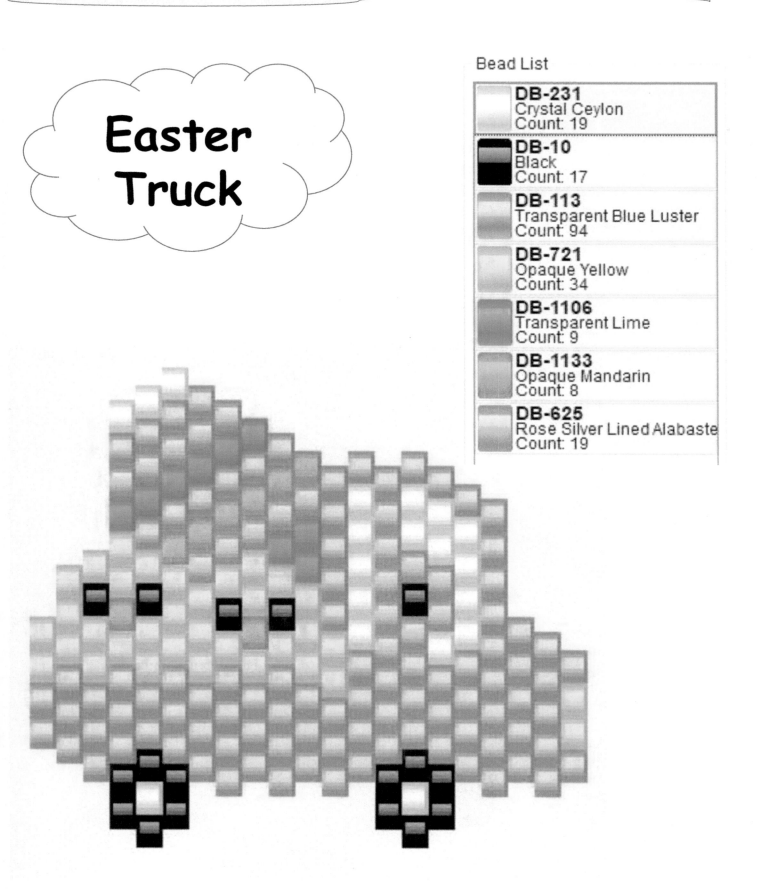

Easter Gnom

Bead List

DB-233
Light Daffodil Ceylon
Count: 13

DB-279
Cranberry Lined Emerald L
Count: 6

DB-246
Dark Cotton Candy Pink Ce
Count: 72

DB-238
Aqua Green Ceylon
Count: 13

DB-231
Crystal Ceylon
Count: 41

DB-113
Transparent Blue Luster
Count: 16

DB-249
Purple Ceylon
Count: 11

Love Gnom

Bead List

DB-246
Dark Cotton Candy Pink Ce
Count: 72

DB-113
Transparent Blue Luster
Count: 6

DB-231
Crystal Ceylon
Count: 36

DB-283
Cranberry Lined Idot Luste
Count: 29

DB-233
Light Daffodil Ceylon
Count: 11

DB-279
Cranberry Lined Emerald L
Count: 6

DB-238
Aqua Green Ceylon
Count: 6

DB-249
Purple Ceylon
Count: 6

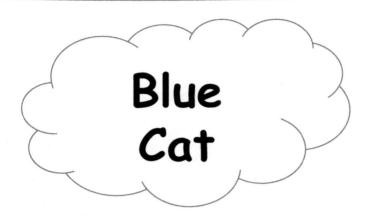

Blue
Cat

Bead List

	DB-10 Black Count: 183	
	DB-57 Aqua Lined Crystal AB Count: 309	
	DB-50 Crystal Luster Count: 12	

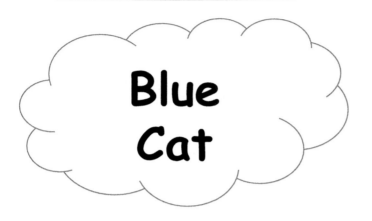

Blue
Cat

Bead List

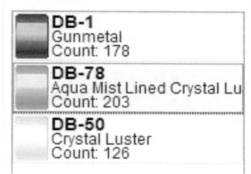

DB-1
Gunmetal
Count: 178

DB-78
Aqua Mist Lined Crystal Lu
Count: 203

DB-50
Crystal Luster
Count: 126

Christmas Reindeer

Bead List

	DB-41	Silver Lined Crystal Count: 134
	DB-42	Silver Lined Gold Count: 134
	DB-44	Silver Lined Aqua Count: 705
	DB-47	Silver Lined Cobalt Count: 223

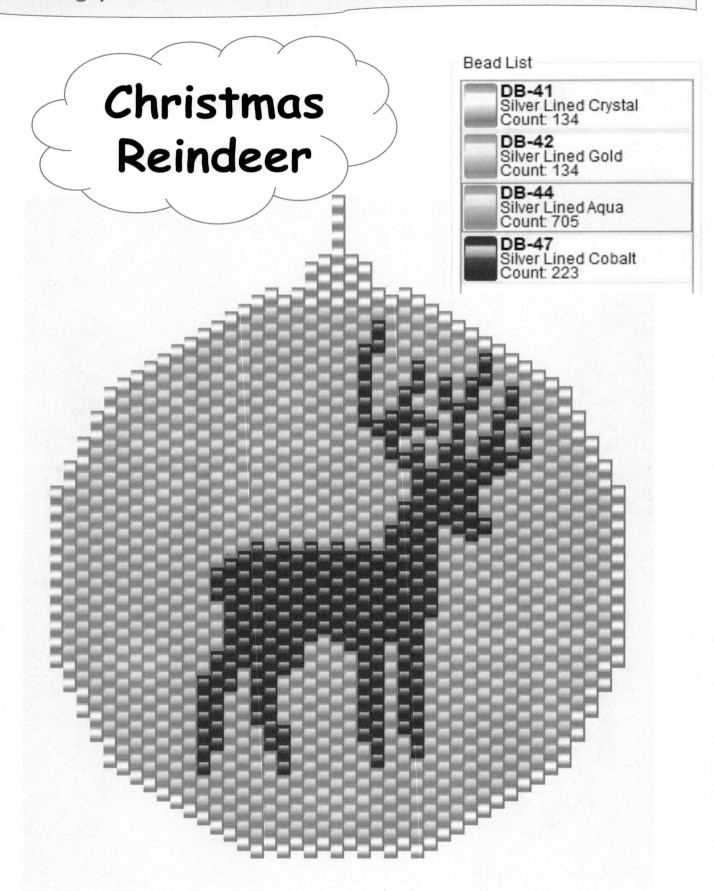

Christmas Snowman

Bead List

	DB-103	Dark Topaz Rainbow Gold Count: 114
	DB-85	Blue Lined Aqua AB Count: 87
	DB-113	Transparent Blue Luster Count: 204
	DB-50	Crystal Luster Count: 779
	DB-10	Black Count: 4
	DB-45	Silver Lined Orange Count: 5

Santa Claus

Bead List

DB-43
Silver Lined Flame Red
Count: 245

DB-10
Black
Count: 2

DB-48
Silver Lined Light Grey
Count: 110

DB-50
Crystal Luster
Count: 339

DB-68
Peach Lined Crystal Luster
Count: 53

DB-70
Coral Lined Crystal Luster
Count: 26

DB-42
Silver Lined Gold
Count: 64

DB-80
Pale Violet Lined Crystal Lu
Count: 358

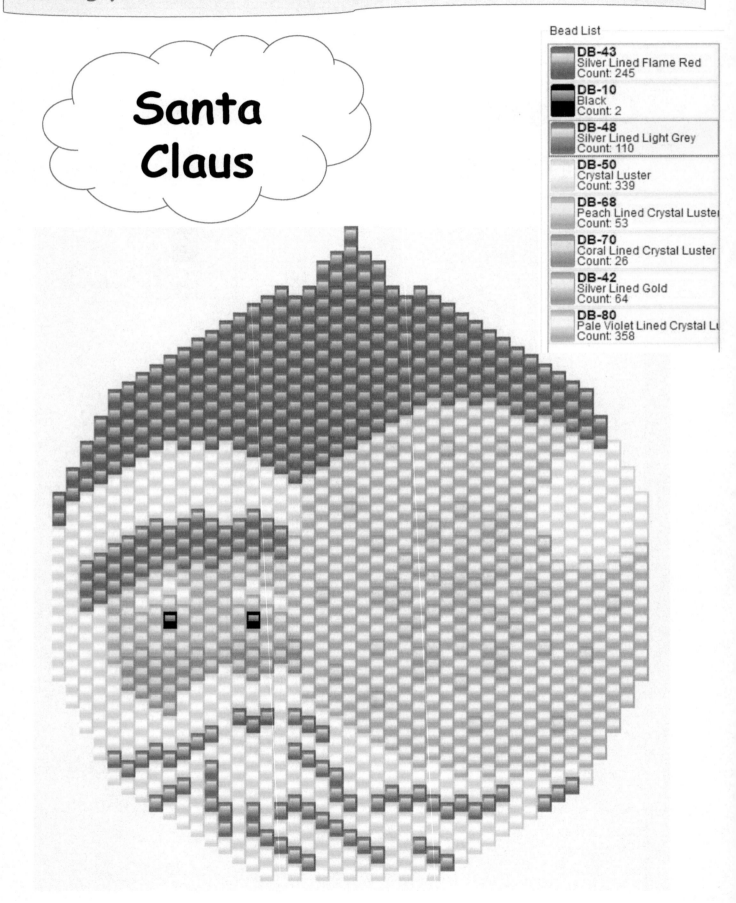

Jesus

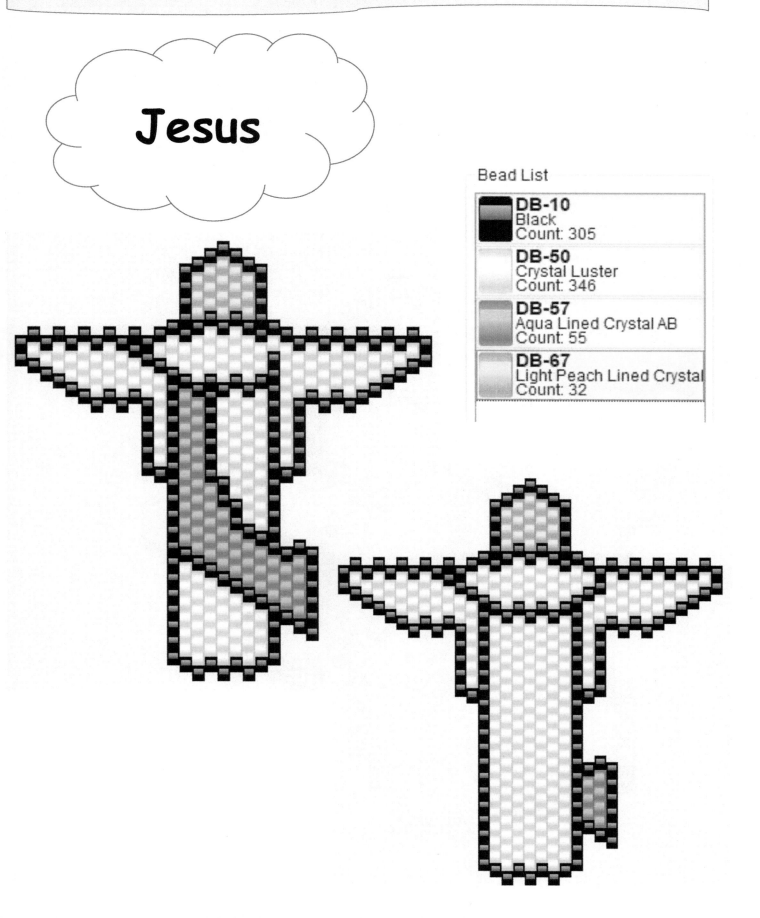

Bead List

	DB-10	Black	Count: 305
	DB-10 Black Count: 305
	DB-50 Crystal Luster Count: 346
	DB-57 Aqua Lined Crystal AB Count: 55
	DB-67 Light Peach Lined Crystal Count: 32

Beading patterns from Natalee Alex

Angel

Bead List

	DB-10 Black Count: 124	
	DB-42 Silver Lined Gold Count: 31	
	DB-50 Crystal Luster Count: 52	
	DB-44 Silver Lined Aqua Count: 118	
	DB-43 Silver Lined Flame Red Count: 13	

Bible

Bead List

	DB-42 Silver Lined Gold Count: 32	
	DB-10 Black Count: 374	
	DB-50 Crystal Luster Count: 352	
	DB-48 Silver Lined Light Grey Count: 239	
	DB-55 Pink Lined Crystal AB Count: 173	

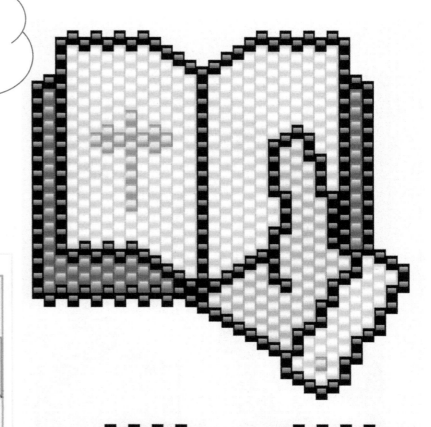

Mother of God

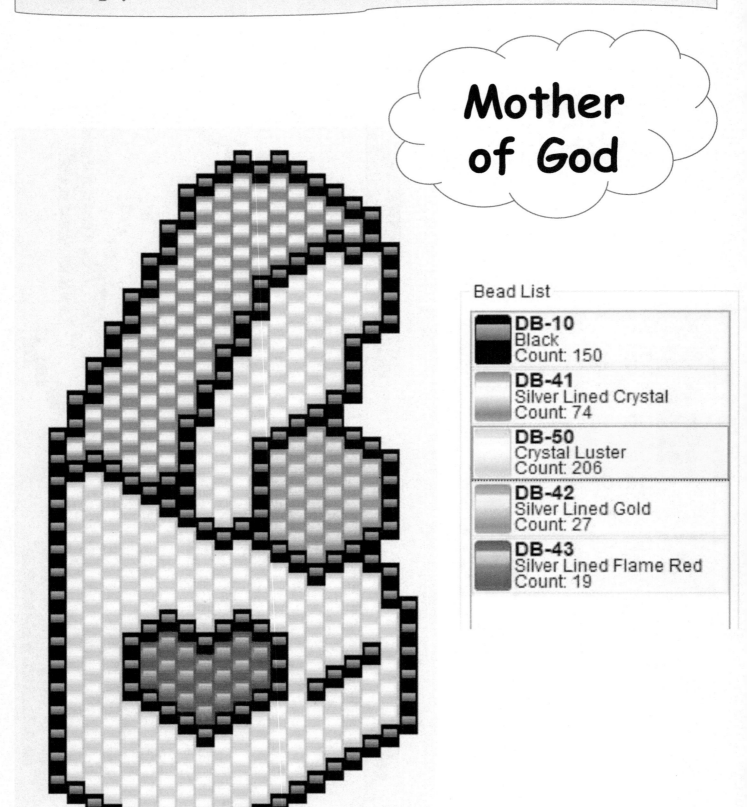

Bead List

	DB-10 Black Count: 150
	DB-41 Silver Lined Crystal Count: 74
	DB-50 Crystal Luster Count: 206
	DB-42 Silver Lined Gold Count: 27
	DB-43 Silver Lined Flame Red Count: 19

Church

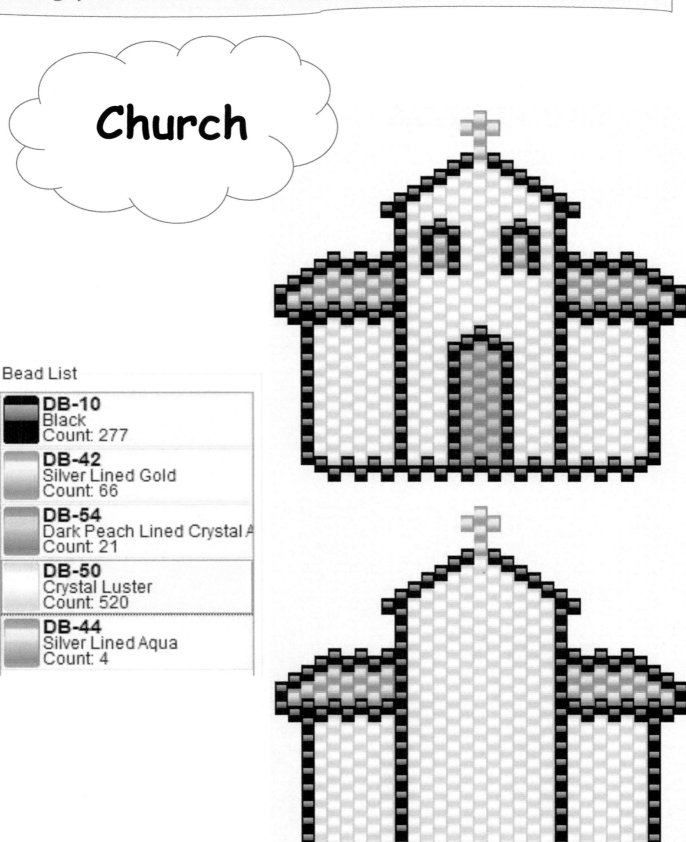

Bead List

DB-10
Black
Count: 277

DB-42
Silver Lined Gold
Count: 66

DB-54
Dark Peach Lined Crystal A
Count: 21

DB-50
Crystal Luster
Count: 520

DB-44
Silver Lined Aqua
Count: 4

Christmas Sock

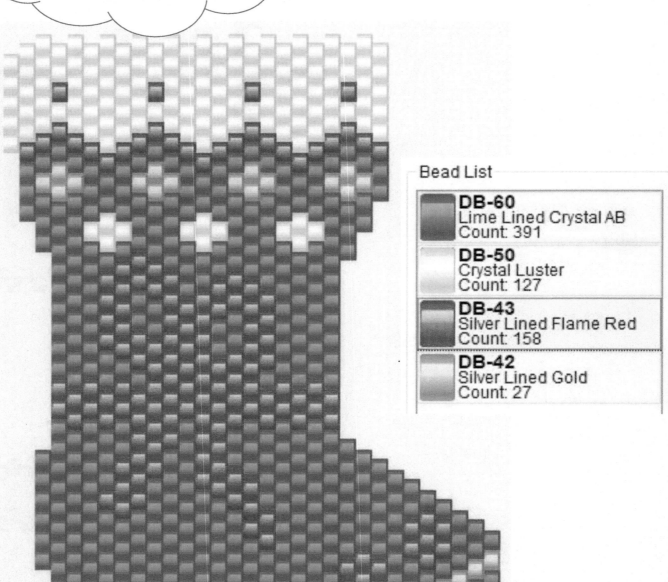

Bead List

	DB-60 Lime Lined Crystal AB Count: 391
	DB-50 Crystal Luster Count: 127
	DB-43 Silver Lined Flame Red Count: 158
	DB-42 Silver Lined Gold Count: 27

Feminist quote

Bead List

DB-10
Black
Count: 250

DB-50
Crystal Luster
Count: 588

Feminist quote

Bead List

	DB-10 Black Count: 175
	DB-50 Crystal Luster Count: 390

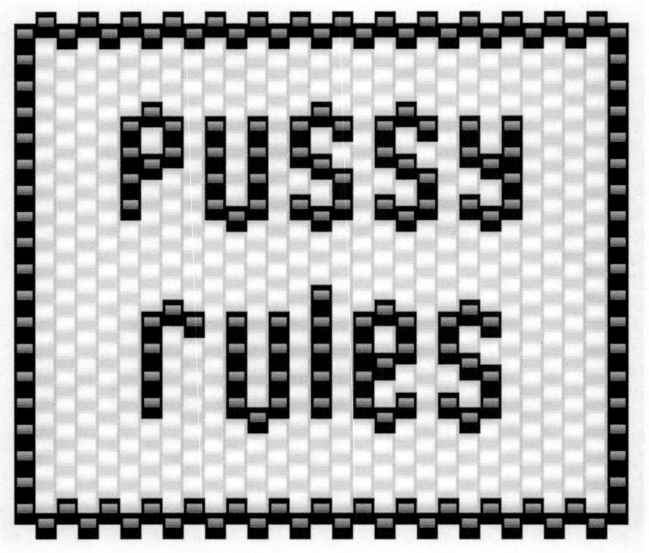

Feminist quote

Bead List

■	**DB-10** Black Count: 230	
□	**DB-50** Crystal Luster Count: 491	

Feminist quote

Bead List

	DB-10	
	Black	
	Count: 269	
	DB-50	
	Crystal Luster	
	Count: 569	

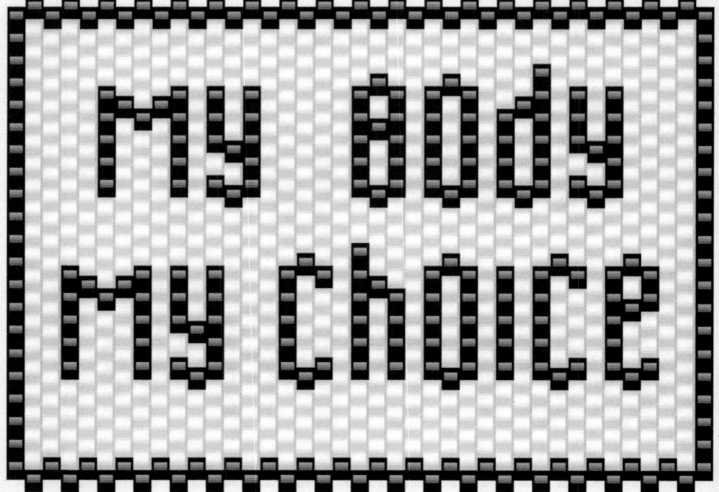

Christmas charms

Bead List

	DB-46 Silver Lined Green Count: 79	
	DB-10 Black Count: 23	
	DB-43 Silver Lined Flame Red Count: 113	
	DB-50 Crystal Luster Count: 179	
	DB-42 Silver Lined Gold Count: 6	
	DB-654 Opaque Maroon Count: 41	
	DB-608 Silver Lined Blue Zircon Count: 87	

Christmas animals

Bead List

DB-42
Silver Lined Gold
Count: 70

DB-53
Light Yellow Lined Crystal
Count: 99

DB-10
Black
Count: 116

DB-43
Silver Lined Flame Red
Count: 72

DB-50
Crystal Luster
Count: 200

DB-45
Silver Lined Orange
Count: 52

DB-48
Silver Lined Light Grey
Count: 44

Girl's charms

Bead List

DB-50
Crystal Luster
Count: 283

DB-1371
Opaque Carnation Pink
Count: 37

DB-149
Silver Lined Capri Blue
Count: 19

DB-42
Silver Lined Gold
Count: 16

DB-169
Opaque Chartreuse AB
Count: 25

DB-158
Opaque Mauve AB
Count: 9

DB-796
Semi-Frosted Opaque Red
Count: 132

DB-10
Black
Count: 96

DB-721
Opaque Yellow
Count: 57

DB-236
Carnation Pink Ceylon
Count: 74

DB-218
Opaque Medium Turquoise
Count: 13

DB-771
Semi-Frosted Transparent
Count: 86

DB-707
Transparent Cobalt
Count: 46

DB-238
Aqua Green Ceylon
Count: 5

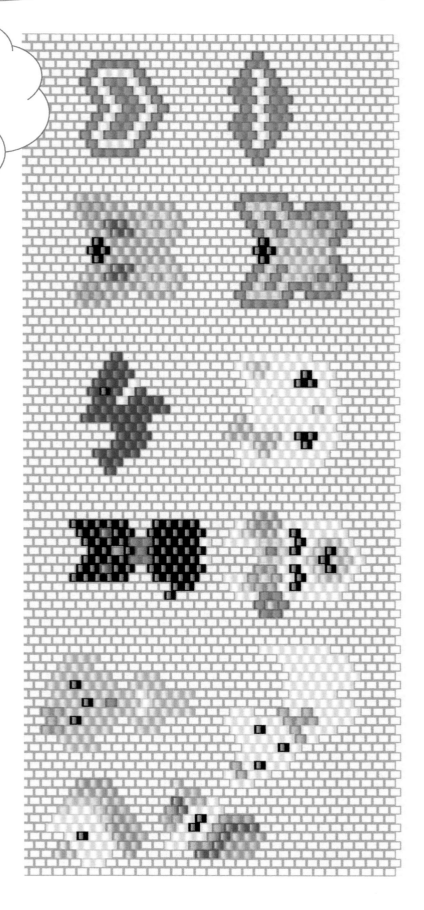

Flower charms

Bead List

DB-50
Crystal Luster
Count: 138

DB-721
Opaque Yellow
Count: 101

DB-771
Semi-Frosted Transparent
Count: 7

DB-42
Silver Lined Gold
Count: 68

DB-1347
Silver Lined Purple
Count: 40

DB-249
Purple Ceylon
Count: 37

DB-902
Sparkling Peony Pink Lined
Count: 93

DB-234
Baby Pink Ceylon
Count: 163

DB-1777
White Lined Orange AB
Count: 7

DB-1848
Galvanized Dusty Orchid D
Count: 59

DB-1855
Color Lined Sun Glow
Count: 6

DB-796
Semi-Frosted Opaque Red
Count: 49

DB-1839
Galvanized Dark Coral Dur
Count: 18

Name project _____ 100x100

Name project _____ 80x80

Name project _____ 50x50

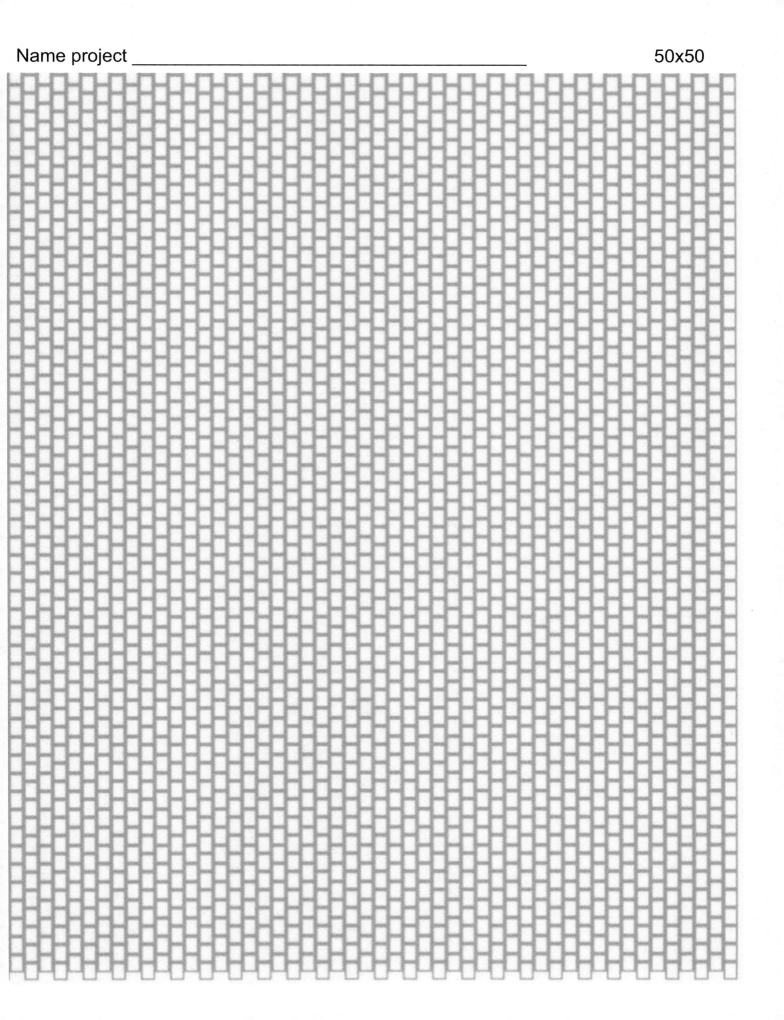

Name project _____ 80x80

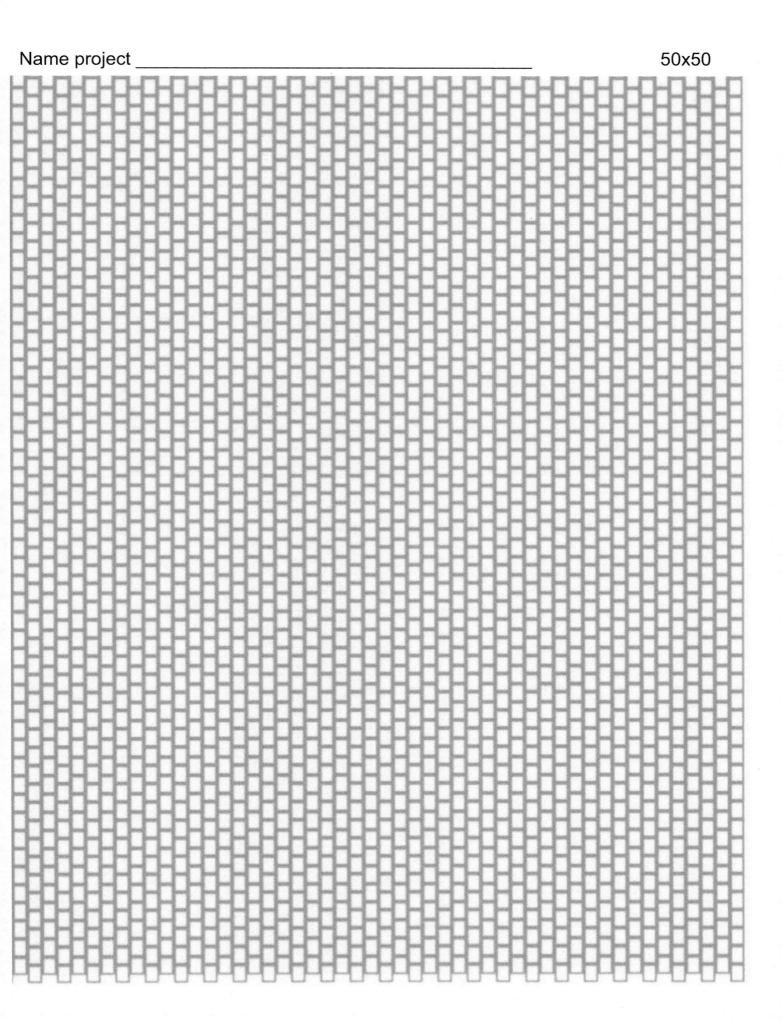

Name project _____ 80x80

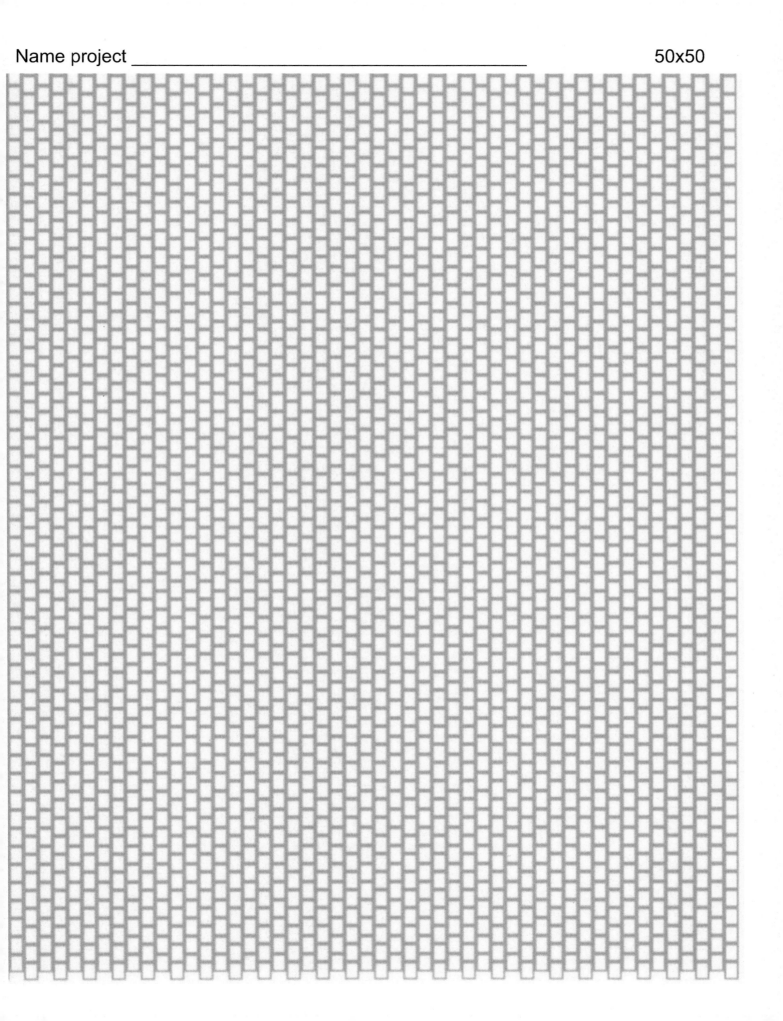

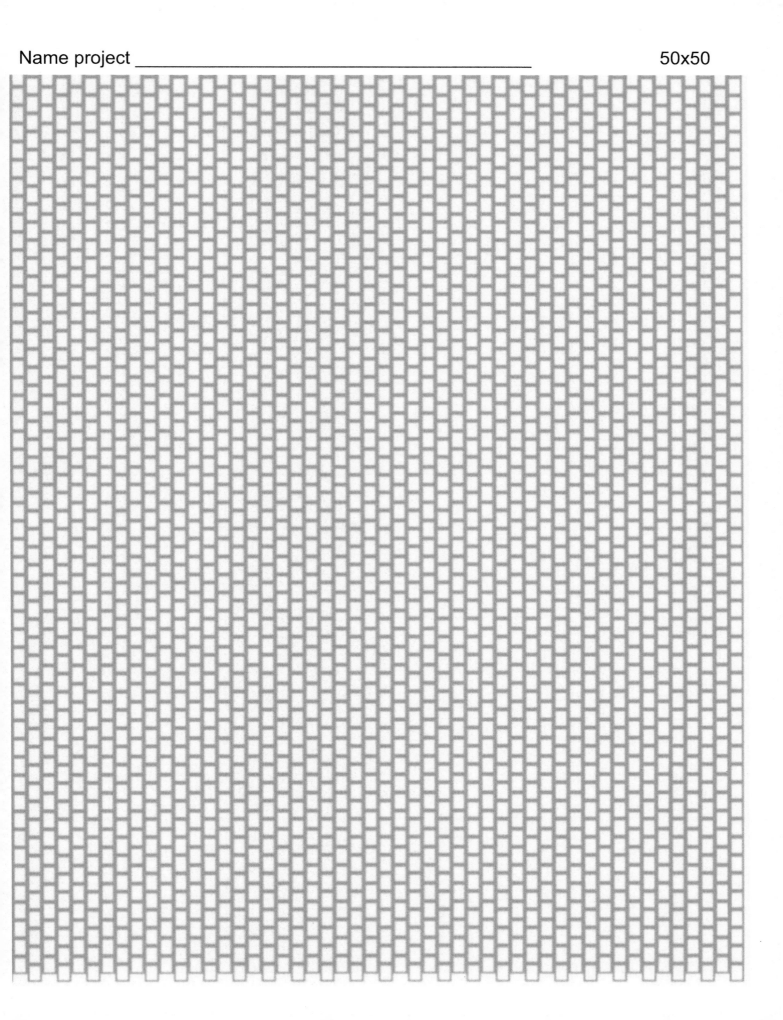

Name project _____

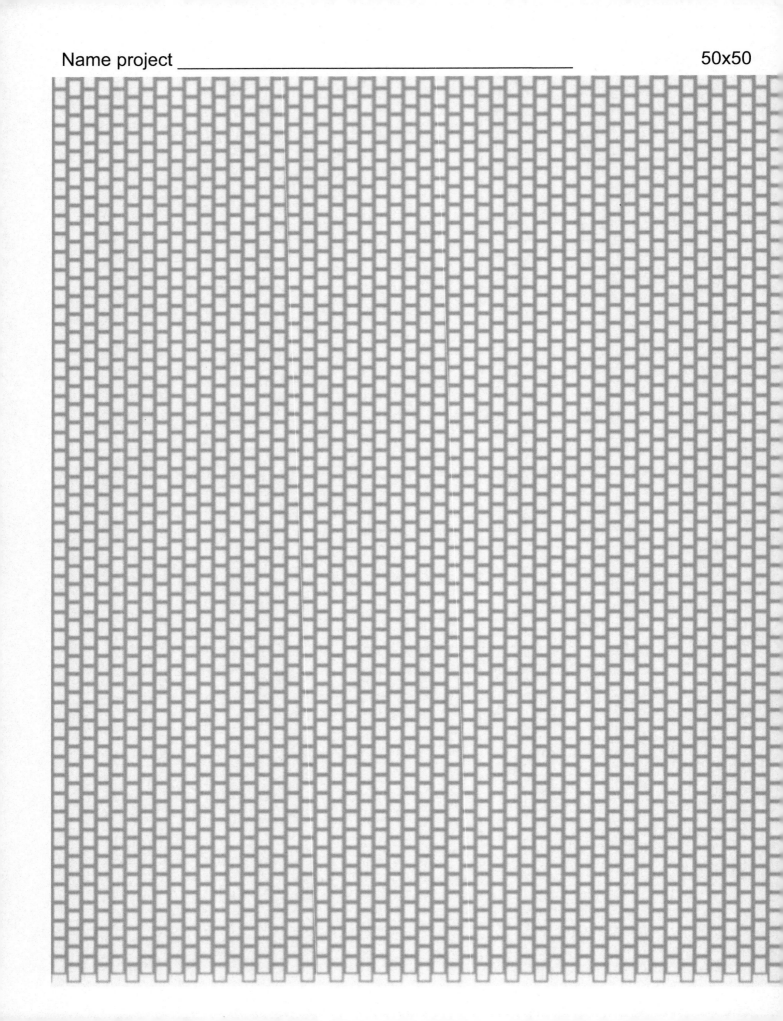

Name project _____ 100x100

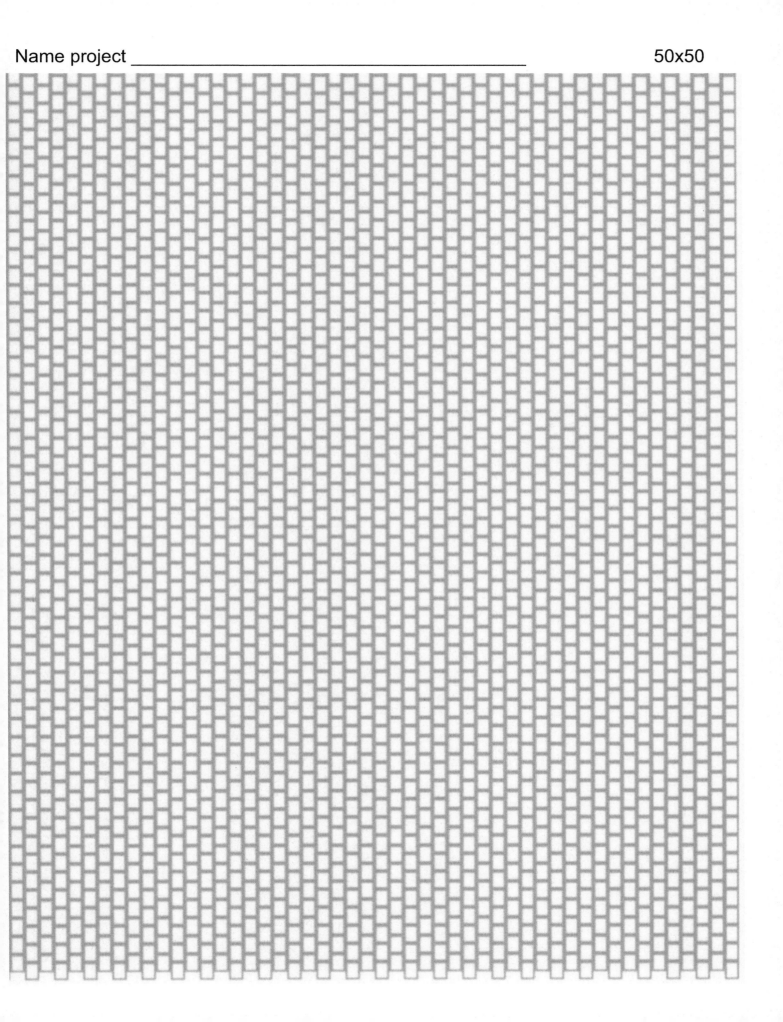

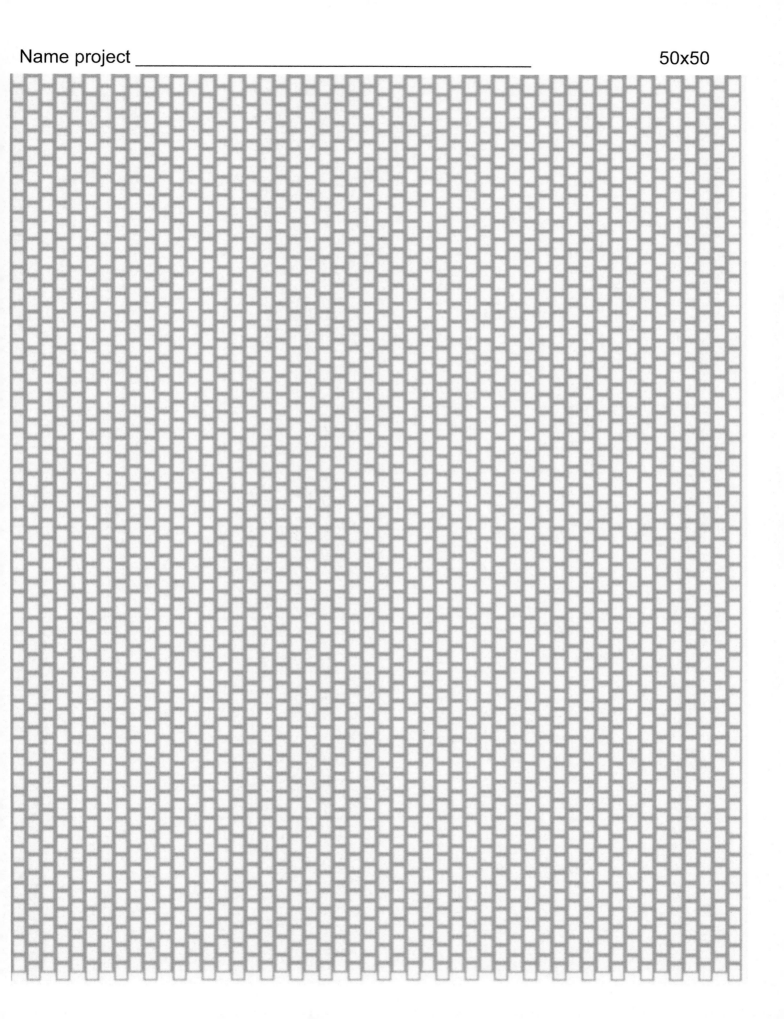

Name project _____ 100x100

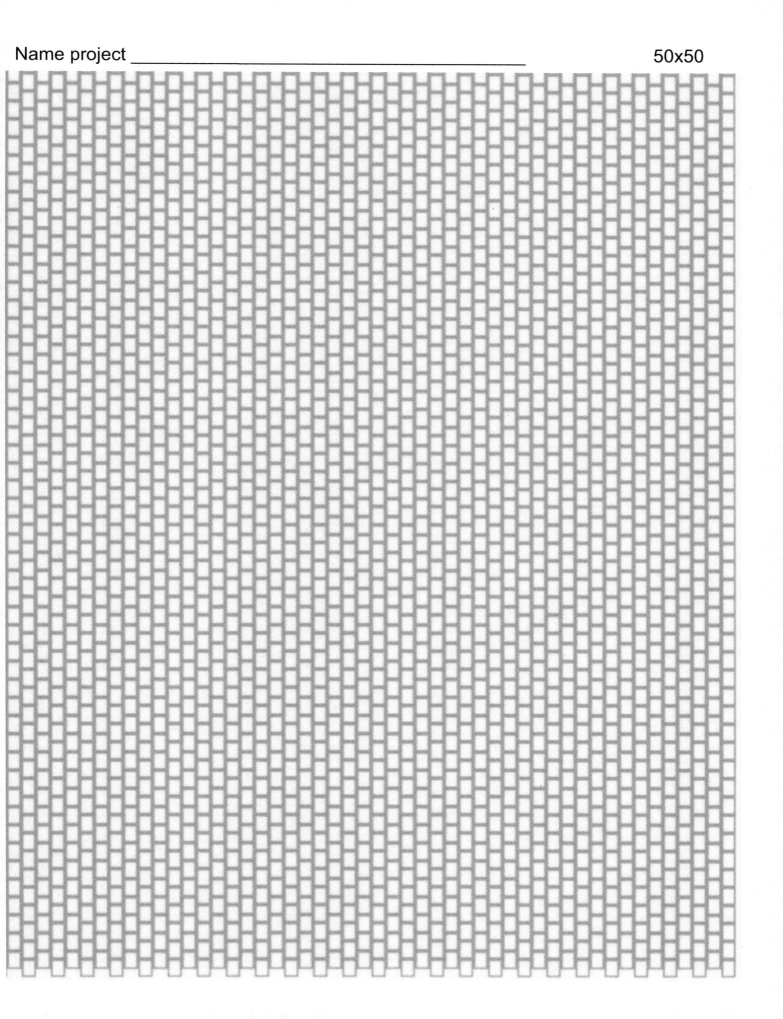

Name project _____ 100x100

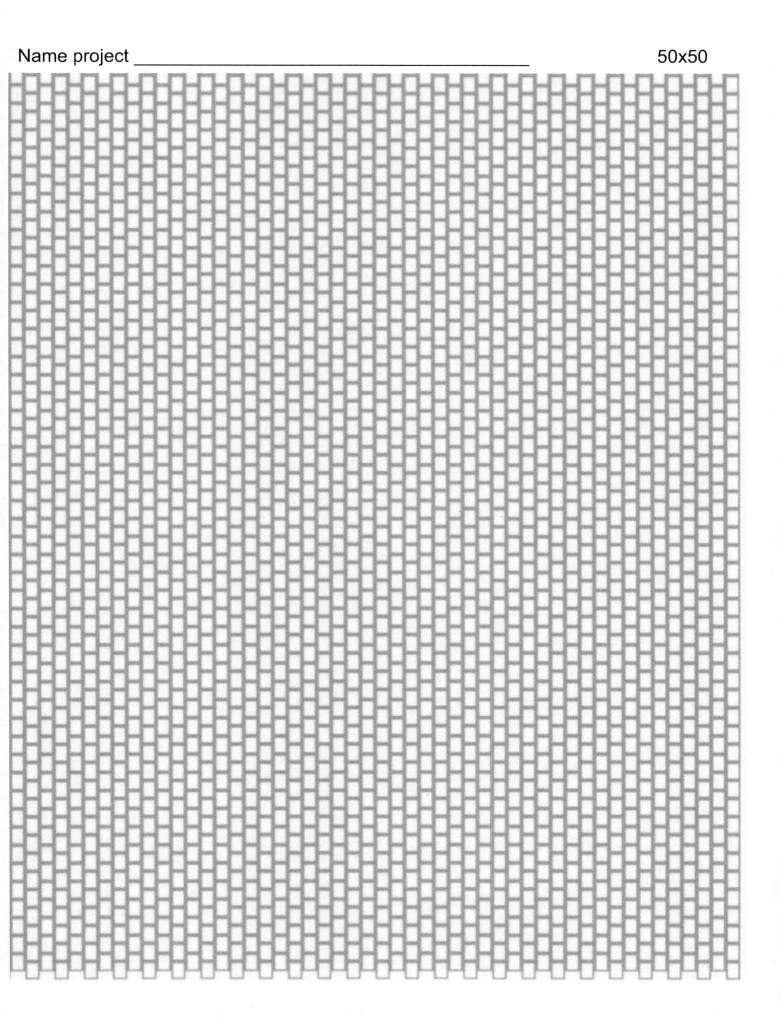

Name project _____ 80x80

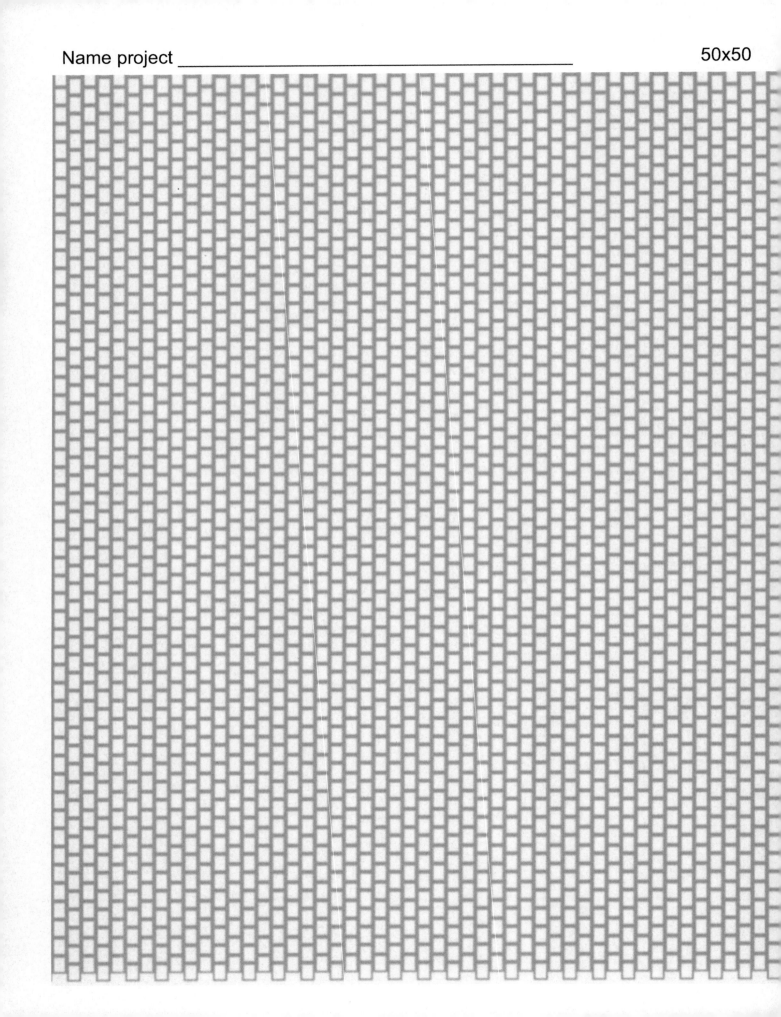

Printed in Great Britain
by Amazon

13396013R00052